SOCCER
SKILLS
& DRILLS

SOCCER
SKILLS
& DRILLS

Ralph Brammer

The Lyons Press
Guilford, Connecticut
An imprint of The Globe Pequot Press

First United States edition © 2003, The Lyons Press

Copyright © 2000 by Elliot Right Way Books

The Lyons Press is an imprint of The Globe Pequot Press

10 9 8 7 6 5 4 3 2 1

Printed in the United States of America

ISBN 1-58574-848-X

Library of Congress Cataloging-in-Publication Data is available on file.

Dedicated to all the youngsters who play soccer and to all the adults who help them. Special thanks to my partner Heather for her input and support, to Ryan Flannery for his role as the pupil, and to Louis Julius for using his skills. Caring thoughts to my late wife Wendy and daughter Lisa: I'm sure they're looking down waiting to see a soccer star evolve from the book.

Acknowledgments to:

James Wilde for the lovely drawings.

My daughter Suzanne and sons Ray, Ryan, and Mark.

Dave Thompson and Craig Roberts for their help.

John Billington for his initial help with photography.

CONTENTS

INTRODUCTION

Soccer has changed much over the years. This once friendly pickup game is now a much sought-after career.

Budding stars now begin soccer at the age of eight or nine, both in school and club games, with thousands more competing in league games each year. All are eager to win titles or trophies and make their way to soccer fame.

Soccer now holds the key to large financial rewards, so parents and youngsters are eager to explore the road to success. Junior levels of soccer are also fun in themselves. Yet no matter what level of soccer you play, and regardless of possible financial gain, there is more purpose and pleasure if you play really well.

Many players of all age groups lack skill. Errors are made in kicking or controlling the ball. Faults often occur with technique, timing, and patience. These faults may give rise to frustration that often leads to aggression or bad habits.

How can a youngster play better? Just look closely at his skills, test his abilities, and know how to bring out the best. Soccer skills such as shooting, passing, ball control, and heading are the essential foundation for success.

The purpose of this book is to show youngsters what to learn, and parents how to teach. The method is a unique plan using a one-on-one formula and step-by-step guide. It is a progressive route to build up confidence and all-around skills. There is due emphasis on speed and timing, so parents can analyze what their child is lacking in, and remedy any shortcomings.

The book does not attempt to cover such aspects as goalkeeping, team tactics, set moves, or rules of the game, but

the final part gives good advice on playing in a team and the
standards to set.

An Important Foundation

Lessons one through five are the basics. They highlight
strengths and weaknesses. They are designed to correct bad
habits and steady a youngster.

Lessons six through fifteen elaborate the fundamentals. They
provide variation on the basic techniques, foster quick thinking,
and coordinate movement. They are designed to increase the
youngster's skill, composure, and confidence with the ball.

Part 2 of the book is a résumé and summary of what every
coach and youngster need to know about The Game.

Fig. 1   The Game at its biggest!

How to Use the Book

Follow the lessons in sequence and from the beginning. This
will set you on the correct path.

It doesn't matter if you can't get into a soccer team, or have
only just started playing, whether you play in a team that
always loses, or one that mostly wins.

You Can Improve Dramatically. How?
From one-on-one teaching lessons
Gain confidence with the ball
Discover balance and timing
Learn to execute skills correctly
Learn to execute skills in the correct sequence
Learn to control and pass the ball with either foot
Learn to shoot and hit the ball long using either foot
Head the ball correctly in attack or defense
Recognize your skills and how to use them
Use your new-found talent on the field

Fig. 2   Gain confidence and show off your skills on the field.

What do I Need?
- A soccer ball.
- A playing field, backyard, or, if necessary, just a hard surface. Don't use your ball too much on a hard surface or you may end up buying a new ball fairly soon.
- A brick wall to practice against. Make sure you are not annoying the neighbors by using their wall.
- Someone to teach you, practice with, and look for good points or mistakes. Mom or Dad will do. Later on, a more skilled person to pass the ball to you. Again, I'm sure a parent will be fine.

Fig. 3   Dad will do nicely.

The Ball

Good low-cost leather balls are available in most sporting goods stores. The ball needs to be a standard size five, or smaller if the child is young. The correct sizes for different ages are:

Ages 7 and under	Size 3
Ages 8 to 12	Size 4
Ages 13 and over	Size 5

Do not pump the ball up too hard, just fairly firm. This is particularly important for younger children. An adult should be able to indent the ball slightly with their thumb.

a

b

Fig. 4   a) The ball.
            b) The shoes.

Your Shoes or Trainers

Your soccer shoes, or trainers, need to be the correct size; above all, they must feel comfortable.

Right from the Start

On average you only have about three minutes of ball possession when playing a full game of soccer. Not a lot, is it? So let's get it right from the start.

Fig. 5   a) Stretching exercises! Cross legs, do not bend knees, try
              touching toes.
           b) Open legs, bend one knee, lean sideways with other leg.
           c) Arms out, slowly turn body from the waist.

Important for Teacher and Pupil: Warm Up First

Light jogging in place and some stretching exercises will do. Please make sure you warm up before any practicing, otherwise you could pull a muscle . . . OUCH! This would more than hinder your soccer for a while. If you are not sure what stretching exercises are, ask your physical education teacher. Fig. 5 shows some stretching exercises in the standing position. Exercise gently and slowly.

For clarity of expression we will from now on use the terms "pupil" and "teacher."

TEACHER:

The First Lessons

The first five lessons are basic, but do not underestimate their value. All players should start off on the right foot, and these lessons may give more of an insight than you expect. So let's see how to perform at the simplest level.

It is sometimes difficult to get through to youngsters, or make them listen; as we all know, most kids think they know best. Be patient and show the child correctly. Then if the child does well at each practice, he will be more confident, and look forward to the next session.

Do not spend too much time on each exercise, but be prepared to go back, try again, and practice regularly. Read the whole section before you start each exercise and take note of the **bold text,** which highlights key aspects. You must, however, spend more time with the first lesson, striking the ball. This will give the pupil a feel for many other skills and set him on the correct path.

PUPIL:

A Side to Encourage

From an early age we all have a tendency to use one particular side of our body for certain tasks. Most of us use our right hand to throw a ball, write, comb our hair, and so on. To stand on a chair, we will always use our stronger foot first to balance. Well, in soccer, these one-sided strengths or weaknesses are detrimental. Problems will occur from not being able to use either foot to strike the ball. This leads to an imbalance in the way you play your game. A "one-footed" soccer player suffers from serious limitations.

LESSON 1

BALANCE AND STRIKING THE BALL

PUPIL: Always strike the ball using the lace area of your shoe. This will ensure you can shoot, hit long passes, and, when experienced, score some real power drives. This method of striking the ball is **vital for you to learn,** and is therefore thoroughly explained.

The first exercise is solely for balance, but will give you
• an insight into striking the ball
• a feel for the movement
• an idea of the action using either foot.
Don't skip these exercises; they will not take up too much time.

See fig. 6a. Balance on your right leg with your **knee slightly bent** and arms out. Lean forward and look down. Bring your other leg backward, **bending your knee,** then forward as if you were kicking a ball. Practice slowly.

Now look at fig. 6b. **Point your toes downward** and imagine kicking the ball **using the lace area of your shoe. Keep your eyes on the spot where you think the ball would be.**

Steady balance is the key. Follow through with your kicking leg, which should end up straight, as in fig. 7a.

Next, try balancing on your right leg, then left leg. Imagine the ball is in place and let your hip swing naturally. Practice until you feel comfortable enough to attempt kicking the ball with the lace area of **either** foot.

Fig. 6   Imagine kicking the ball.

Fig. 7   a) A good follow-through.
b) And try the other foot.

First Learn to Strike a Ball

PUPIL: Place your right kicking foot (lace area) up to the ball with **knee bent and toes pointing down.** Look at fig. 8a. Your eyes should be on the ball. Now turn your heel **very slightly inward.** Fig. 8b shows the position exactly. You now have your kicking foot in the correct position to strike the ball. Your standing foot **should be alongside the ball** (about 3 inches away), **pointing in the direction you want the ball to go.** Keep practicing this position many times with both your left and right foot.

Fig. 8   a) Correct position of contact.
b) Heel inward.

Preparing to Strike the Ball

PUPIL: Take up the same position again. Now bend your knee and bring your foot away from the ball about 8 inches, as in fig. 9a. Wait a moment. Now, with the lace area of your shoe, gently strike the ball, as in fig, 9b. Practice this with your **left and right foot alternately. For now, always strike the ball with the center of your foot and hit the middle part of the ball. This will enable you to direct the ball straight and low when it leaves your foot, as in fig. 10. Always keep your eye on the ball.**

a   b

Fig. 9   Striking the ball.

Now Strike the Ball Slightly More Firmly

PUPIL: Take up the same position, but bring your leg and foot further back and execute the strike in one complete steady movement. As your foot **nears** the ball, **increase the speed of your foot** and strike the ball with a **quick, sharp tap.** The sequence is shown in fig. 11. Always look closely at the ball. As your foot nears the ball, increase the speed of your foot. Feel the ball leaving the lace area of your foot. If your foot makes correct contact the ball will travel quite fast without much effort, so you don't need to strike the ball hard.

Fig. 10   Imagine kicking the ball.

Fig. 11   Hit it a bit harder.

You **must** use your right foot, and then left foot, and so on, especially at this stage.

TEACHER: Tell the pupil, "take your time, eye on the ball, gentle strike" (strike meaning use the lace of your shoe). Watch the pupil's performance while giving instructions.

Hit the Target

PUPIL: Place a target on the floor, about 6–7 yards in front of you. Approach the ball from behind, but slightly to one side, and kick it to hit the target using your right foot and then your left, as shown in fig. 12. **Bend your knees and keep your eye on the ball. Use a steady leg action with a slightly quicker strike.** You may feel awkward striking the ball with your left and then right foot. However, keep trying and you will get there. **Accuracy is the key at this stage, not whacking the ball!** Power comes later.

Fig. 12   Ready to walk and strike the ball.
Right foot strike.
Left foot strike.

TEACHER: Remind the pupil, **"take your time, eye on the ball, gentle strike."** Tell the pupil to practice the approach sequence of striking the ball, but **stop his foot just as it is about to strike the ball.** This will enable both you and the pupil to see any faults. To ensure the pupil hits the middle part of the ball, remind him to **"fix your eyes on a point at the middle of the ball."** Looking at a central point on the ball will give a guiding effect.

A typical miss results from the pupil:
• not keeping his eye on the ball
• not placing the non-kicking foot to the side of the ball
• not hitting the middle part of the ball.

More Right and Left Foot Accuracy

PUPIL: Place two smaller targets 6–8 feet on either side of the main target, as in fig. 13. Stand behind the ball and aim at these new targets. Practice the left foot, then the right foot, and repeat.

Fig. 13   Practice again with additional smaller targets.

TEACHER: We now see a change from the last exercise to give the pupil a different feel for the ball. This is a useful test of timing and accuracy.

Stand facing the pupil. Now throw the ball underhand gently towards the pupil's right or left foot, allowing the ball to bounce once or twice before reaching him. The pupil uses first his left then right foot in turn to strike the ball gently back to you. Remind the pupil, **"take your time, eye on the ball, gentle strike—"** again, striking with the lace area of the shoe.

Fig. 14   Throw the ball directly onto the pupil's foot.

Now move closer to the pupil and **throw the ball directly onto his left or right foot,** as in fig. 14. The pupil should gently strike the ball back to you, **low into your arms.** Throw the ball accurately and you will find that this is a good test for the youngster.

Useful Practice on your Own

PUPIL: Follow the sequence shown in fig. 15. Drop the ball in front of you, let it bounce one time, then gently strike it against a wall. When the ball returns, let it bounce on the ground, then, using the other foot, gently strike it back against the wall. **Use the lace area of your shoe and keep the ball low. Use your right foot and then left foot and then repeat until you build up a continuous flow.** Keep a steady rhythm **by repositioning yourself quickly for the bounce.** If you can't keep the flow going, stop the ball and start again.

Fig. 15   Kicking the ball against a wall.

More Practice on Your Own—Strike the Ball Low and Get a Feel for the Action

PUPIL: Stand 6–8 feet away from a wall. Place one foot **alongside** the ball, then strike it against the wall, as in fig. 16. See if you can make the ball travel close to the ground and come back to you fairly accurately. Trap the ball using the inside of your foot and start again. Practice first with your **right** foot, then use your **left**. **Lean slightly forward with your arms out for balance and keep your eye on the ball.** Next, you are going to strike the ball while it is moving:
* Strike the ball back and forth off the wall using only your **right** foot. You will need to **move quickly into a good**

Fig. 16   Strike the ball low with the right foot . . .

position to strike the returning ball. Hit the middle to top part of the ball to keep it low.
- Now try using only your left foot to strike the ball back and forth off the wall, as in fig. 17.
- Next, strike the ball back and forth off the wall using alternate feet.

Fig. 17 . . . and then the left foot. Move quickly to strike the returning ball.

LESSON 2

TRAPPING AND CONTROLLING THE BALL WITH YOUR FEET

We will return to striking techniques, but for now let's move on to the second lesson: how to control the ball and produce the right effect. It is easier to control a ball on the ground than one in the air, however we don't want to make things too easy for you.

PUPIL: The best way to control a ball at waist level or below is to use the inside of your foot. Judge where the ball will land and place your foot accordingly, or bring your foot up in the air. The ball should end up on the ground, in front of you.

Sounds easy? Then why do we see so many errors on a soccer field, especially at lower levels? **You must be in control of the ball—do not let the ball control you.** Do not chase after the ball frantically if you make a mistake. This is a waste of energy and only indicates the need to practice.

TEACHER: Stand facing the pupil, 6–8 feet away from her. Throw the ball so it lands on the **inside** of the pupil's right foot, as shown in fig. 18. Now do the same with the left foot. Throw the ball low to the ground, varying up to waist level, and call out **"eye on the ball."**

PUPIL: Keep your eye on the ball and relax. Bring your foot back at the **same speed as the ball** to cushion it at the

Fig. 18   If your foot remains rigid, the ball will bounce from it. Bring your
foot back at the same speed as the ball to cushion it.

Fig. 19   Control a high ball by lifting your foot up and back to cushion
the ball. The ball then drops to the ground.

moment of impact. If the action is correct, the ball will then
drop near to your feet, as in fig. 19.

TEACHER: Once the pupil has learned this technique, gradually increase the distance between you. Walk backward 2 feet at a time, and throw the ball again. From now on, as soon as the pupil makes contact with the ball, call **"head up." The pupil needs to look up without delay** (see fig. 20). Tell the pupil to strike the ball back to you gently, using alternate feet. Tell her to "take your time, eye on the ball" and so on. Repeat this until you are 18–20 feet away from her.

Fig. 20   After contact with the ball, call "Head Up."

Build up to a Quicker Reaction with Steady Ball Control

TEACHER: Always throw or kick the ball fairly accurately to the pupil. You may need to pass the ball along the ground if the pupil is young, but still tell her to bring her foot back to cushion the force of the ball.

Using the exercise above, face the pupil, 7–10 yards away from her. The pupil should turn her head and look either to the left or to the right (see fig. 21). Throw or kick the ball to the pupil and, at the same time, call **"control."** The pupil needs to respond quickly, look at the ball, move if necessary, and then control the ball using the inside of her foot. Afterwards, tell her, **"head up"** and then she should gently strike the ball back to you.

a   b

Fig. 21 The pupil waits for the teacher's command.

- Now do the same exercise, but first tell the pupil which foot to trap the ball with.
- Now do the same exercise again, but this time tell the pupil which side to turn to.

Useful Practice—Trapping the Ball on your Own

PUPIL: Drop the ball in front of you. Gently strike the ball against a wall using your right foot, as in fig. 22. When the ball bounces back, control it using the inside of your left foot, as in fig. 23.

Fig. 22   Strike the ball with the right foot . . .

Fig. 23   . . . and trap the ball with the left foot.

Now strike the ball with your left foot, trapping it with your right, and so on.

LESSON 3
BASIC AWARENESS

You will have more practice trapping the ball later on, but for now let's try something different.

It is very important for players to know what's going on around them. Imagine being in the center of a soccer field, watching a game with fast action in the midfield area. This back-and-forth movement could make you dizzy. A player will turn many times in a game, and so it is important to practice circular movements. The following exercises will improve the pupil's perception and orientation, while at the same time increasing his confidence with the ball at his feet.

PUPIL: Walk in an imaginary 20–30 foot diameter circle (see fig. 24c) with the ball at your feet. As in figs. 24a and 24b, keep your **head up, look ahead, left and right, only glancing at the ball briefly.** Use alternate feet to control the ball, keeping it close to you at all times. Now turn and walk the circle in the other direction.

Jogging the Circle

Jog the same circle with the ball but, halfway around, stop the ball by planting the sole of your shoe on it, as in fig. 25a. Now turn quickly and take the ball the other way. Keep your **head up** and keep the ball close to you.

Practice this a few times and slowly build up speed without losing possession of the ball. **Do not run too fast** as this may make you dizzy.

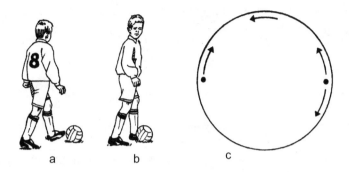

Fig. 24 a) Look ahead with the ball at your feet . . .
b) . . .look to the right and the left too.
c) Walk a 25–30 foot diameter circle.

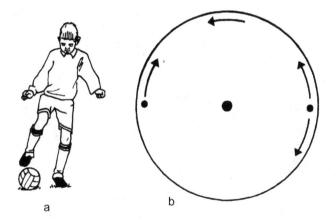

Fig. 25 a) Stop the ball with the sole of your shoe.
b) The teacher stands at the center of the circle. When he calls "turn," the pupil changes his direction and takes the ball the other way.

TEACHER: Look at fig. 25b. Stand in the middle of the imaginary circle. From time to time, reverse the direction that the pupil jogs by giving the command **"turn."** Now tell the pupil to stop the ball using alternate feet: give the commands **"left foot turn"** or **"right foot turn."** Call **"head up"** after each turn.

Be Aware of What's Going on Around you—Feel the Ball at your Feet

PUPIL: Jog around the same circle again, but this time stop at each half of the circle. Face the center of the circle, place one foot on top of the ball and pivot backwards in a small circle, as illustrated in figs. 26a and 26b. Use the sole of your shoe to guide the ball around with you. For counterclockwise circles, use your left foot on the ball; for clockwise circles, use your right foot. After turning on the spot, you should end up facing the center of the larger circle again. **Keep your head up** while controlling the ball.

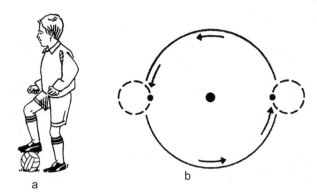

Fig. 26   a) The teacher calls "stop" . . .
               b) . . .and the pupil rolls the ball backward as he pivots in a small circle.

TEACHER: Stand in the middle of the circle and give the command **"stop."** Now tell the pupil which foot to use to roll the ball.

Small Forward Circles

PUPIL: As before, jog the circle, in either direction, with the ball at your feet. At each half of the circle, take the ball in a small forward circle and continue on in the same direction as before (figs. 27a and 27b). Practice the small circles counterclockwise then clockwise. Control the ball using the **inside** of your feet. Keep your head up and only glance at the ball now and again.

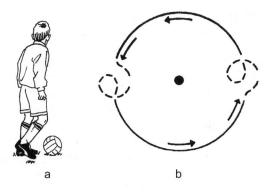

a   b

Fig. 27   The pupil takes the ball in a small forward circle, then continues in the same direction as before.

TEACHER: As the pupil reaches the halfway point of the circle, give the command **"small circle"** and indicate whether it is to be clockwise or counterclockwise.

LESSON 4
HEADING THE BALL

We will return to circle moves again but, for now, another lesson.

PUPIL: This exercise is the basis from which you can develop your heading skills. Stand facing a wall, about one yard away from it. Using both hands, hold the ball up to the **center** of your forehead, well clear of your nose. With your **eyes open,** bring your head back and arch your back. Now strike the ball out of your hands, against the wall, with your forehead. Practice this until you can recognize which part of your forehead you need to use and how bringing your head back gives power and direction to the ball.

Now imagine that the ball is coming to you from your right. Turn your body slightly to the right and place your left foot forward, as in fig. 28. You can still head the ball forward with your body facing another way because you are directing the ball **with your forehead,** which should be facing **towards the wall.** Next, imagine the ball is coming from the left by placing your right foot forward and heading the ball.

Practice Other Headers

You can use this method to practice other headers, for example a high ball. Hold the ball higher and look up, as in fig. 29a. Bring the ball towards your forehead and, at the same time, arch your back. Now attack the ball with your forehead (fig. 29b).

Fig. 28 Turn to the right with your left foot forward. Keep the ball at the center of your forehead.

a   b

Fig. 29 a) Hold the ball high and look up . . .
b) . . .the ball is returned high in the air by the direction and power of your forehead.

Build up your Confidence in Heading the Ball

PUPIL: When the ball is traveling fast, the timing of your forehead contact is very important, but you will need time to practice this. **Always keep your eyes open and meet the ball with your forehead.** You may blink naturally on contact with the ball, but you should always be able to see where the ball is coming from and, afterwards, where it is going (don't miss seeing your goal go in!).

TEACHER: Stand facing the pupil, 3–4 yards away. Gently throw the ball underhand, and slightly higher than her head. The pupil should then head the ball back to you, using the same technique as with the wall practice. Tell her to head the ball back to you, first at eye level (fig. 30), and then progressively higher in the air.

Fig. 30   Heading the ball back at eye level.

Vary the Headers

Now tell the pupil to head the ball towards the right or the left. Let her head the ball towards a wall—this will give her a target to aim at, and will save time in collecting the ball.

   Now tell the pupil whether to head the ball high (fig. 31) or low, and throw the ball from either side of the pupil (fig. 32).

Fig. 31 Heading the ball higher.

Increase the Distance

Still throwing underhand, slightly increase the distance between you and the pupil. If you are in any doubt about the pupil's performance, go back to some simpler headers and work up to the harder exercises again.

Fig. 32   Heading the ball down.

LESSON 5

THE SIDE-FOOT PASS

We now move on to passing the ball, using the inside of your foot. You can practice this after the stretching exercises, and while warming up. The following method is fairly straightforward, although very different from striking the ball. Do not try anything fancy at this stage.

TEACHER: Demonstrate the following kick to the pupil, making sure to emphasize the difference between side-foot passing and striking the ball. The pupil must use alternate feet.

PUPIL: Walk up to the ball from almost directly behind it and turn your **right foot outward to make a right angle with your left foot,** as shown in fig. 33. **Use the area of the side of your foot midway between the toe and the heel to kick the ball with a fast lower leg movement** (fig. 34). Moving your foot fast means that you hit the ball harder. **Hit the middle of the ball so that it will travel straight and low.** Practice against a wall to see what level of accuracy and firmness you can achieve. Use your right, then your left foot and so on.

Using your Left and Right Foot
PUPIL: Have you seen some of the great players take penalties? Well, try this. With your teacher as goalkeeper, place the ball on the penalty spot and walk back 2–3 yards,

Fig. 33   Turn your foot to make a right angle with the other foot.

Fig. 34   Keeping your eye on the ball, pass the ball with a fast, hard tap.

directly behind the ball (fig. 35). Stop. Look at where you will aim your shot (low, and about 2–3 feet inside the post). Now jog up to the ball. Place one foot alongside the ball, keep your eye on the ball, then side-foot the ball in the same manner as you have been practicing. Practice using your left and right foot, but also aim on either side of the goalkeeper. These variations are not easy.

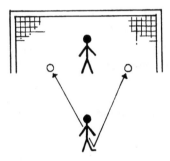

Fig. 35   Practice using your right and left foot.

AN INTRODUCTION TO THE SECOND SET OF LESSONS

PUPIL:
- Have you practiced all the skills in lessons 1 through 5?
- How confident are you?
- Can you execute the skills correctly?
- Have you improved?

If in any doubt, practice more before you continue . . .

If you were to compare a local league soccer game with a National League game, you'd see that there is a great variation in the levels of skill exhibited. However, the physical aspects of play may differ little at times. Some of the players in the lower league teams may be able to match the straightforward running speed of the National League players.

Whether or not he can run fast, a soccer player's priority must be the development of his skills. The longer you leave it, the harder these skills are to acquire. The more you rely on your speed as a youngster, the less likely you are to control your speed when you are older. The best way to play is with quick, agile ball control, or short bursts of speed, but first you will need to focus more on your technique.

TEACHER: Youngsters need help in nurturing their abilities. This involves patience and the teaching of discipline. All children have a tendency to get excited when they run around with the ball, often quickly losing interest and becoming bored. At times, you will need to remain calm and add some fun into the practice. Children are able to learn things more quickly than adults, so make sure you explain the procedures correctly in order to build a good foundation for when they are older.

The next lessons will highlight the need to practice hard. Do not spend too much time on any one lesson. Go through each exercise three or four times before moving on, but be prepared to go back and repeat the whole sequence. If he is eager, the pupil will want to go back and perfect all the lessons anyway. The lessons are in a set sequence, so avoid skipping ahead. As you warm up, recap some of the previous lessons.

PUPIL: If you are currently playing for a team, read the final part of the book before you play your next game. This will help you to understand how to play steadily in a game and also what you are supposed to be doing on the field.

We now move on to the next set of lessons. Some of these will need a reasonably competent person who can kick the ball and perform tricks, like handstands and cartwheels. No, only joking!

LESSON 6

STRIKING THE BALL WITH GREATER PRECISION

PUPIL: Stand facing a wall, about 15–20 feet away from it. (Now tap your foot on the ground impatiently, while your teacher is reading the next section.) You will strike the ball from the same position throughout this lesson. You may notice that the phrase "gentle strike" has disappeared; however, if you miss the target, go back to striking gently. Remember: power comes later! **Use the center (lace area) of your shoe to strike the middle part of the ball, or just above.** This will help keep the ball low. The position of your foot also guides the ball low, so **point your toes down**. As always, keep your eye on the ball.

TEACHER: Stand nearer than the pupil is to the wall, but to one side of her. Facing the pupil, pass a ball along the ground towards her, as shown in fig. 36. The pupil should then strike the moving ball and shoot at the target area on the wall. Pass the ball from the pupil's **right side** so that she uses her **right foot to strike the ball.** Now pass the ball from the pupil's **left side** so that she uses her **left foot to strike the ball** (fig. 37). Do not vary the procedure with this lesson.

Receiving a Pass From the Side
TEACHER: Both you and the pupil should stand 15–20 feet away from a wall, and about 10–12 feet apart from each other.

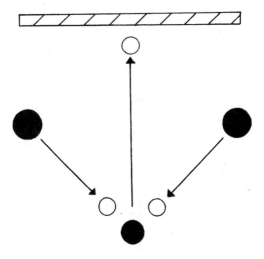

Fig. 36   Teacher passes the ball. Pupil shoots at the target.

Fig. 37   The teacher passes from the left side . . . and the pupil shoots
with his left foot. Strike the middle to top part of the ball to keep
it low.

Pass the ball to the pupil, as in fig. 38. The pupil now receives the ball from the side and should strike it against the wall. Pass the ball from either side of the pupil. When being passed a ball from her right side, the pupil should use her right foot to strike; when passed from the left, she should use his left foot to hit the ball, as in fig. 39.

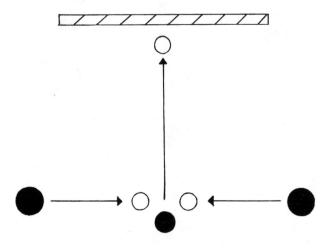

Fig. 38   Teacher passes ball from either side. Pupil shoots the ball forward.

Fig. 39   A pass from the left side—the pupil uses his left foot to strike the ball.

Receiving a Pass From the Rear
TEACHER: Now stand slightly behind the pupil, but still to one side (fig. 40). Pass the ball from the pupil's right (as in fig. 41) and left side as before. The pupil needs to strike the ball low and precisely into the goal. Remind her, "eye on the ball—strike!"

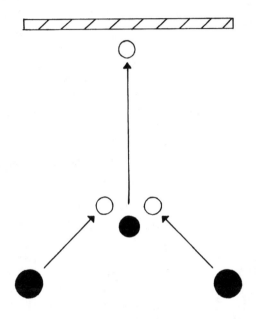

Fig. 40   Teacher passes the ball from slightly behind the pupil.

This exercise makes it more difficult for the pupil to strike a moving ball. It is good practice for his balance and timing, and it tests his ability to strike the ball using either foot.

The Half Volley
For this, the pass needs to be accurate and the strike somewhat faster. This type of exercise will show the importance of correct timing and precision, as well as the need for quick

Fig. 41   Teacher passes the ball from the right side. The pupil strikes the
ball low, using his right foot.

reflex actions. For the moment, only spend a short time on this
exercise.

TEACHER: Take up the same positions as in the previous
exercise, but move closer to the pupil. Throw the ball
underhand toward the pupil's foot, **allowing the ball to hit the
ground just before reaching his foot.** The pupil should then
use a **short but swift strike** to hit the ball against the wall.
   Throw the ball from all six positions, as in fig. 42. Tell the
pupil to **arch her body** over the ball, keeping her **toes down**
and her **eye on the ball.**

PUPIL: Immediately after the ball bounces up, strike it
towards the wall. You must use your left or right foot,
depending on what side the ball comes to you from. Look for
the bounce then execute a **short swift strike,** as in fig. 43. This
will give you a feel for the quick lower leg movement which
provides accuracy with some power.

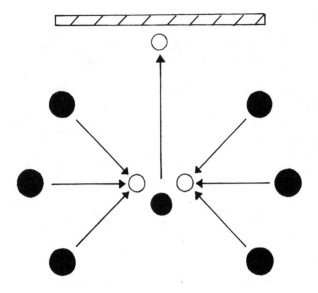

Fig. 42   Teacher throws the ball from all six positions.

Fig. 43   Teacher throws the ball to hit the ground just before it reaches the pupil's foot.

Full Volleys in the Six Positions

TEACHER: Take up the same position as in the previous exercise, but **move a lot closer to the pupil.** Throw the ball underhand so that it lands directly onto the pupil's foot. She should then strike the ball low into the goal. Throw the ball gently and accurately from all six positions, three either side of the pupil, as shown in fig. 44. The pupil must execute all of these strikes correctly (at least once) before she moves on.

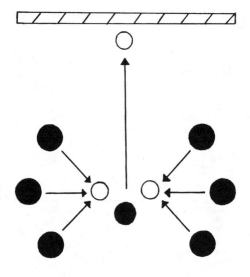

Fig. 44   Teacher moves closer and throws the ball from all six positions.

PUPIL: Your shot needs to be low. Anybody can whack a ball in the air! **You need to use the lace area of your shoe, but aim low so the ball travels either level or towards the ground,** as in fig. 45.

Fig. 45   Teacher throws the ball so it lands on the pupil's foot.
Pupil strikes the ball low into the goal.

TEACHER: From the last three exercises you can now judge the pupil's ability to strike the ball. These are good tests of skill, some difficult to execute. If the pupil has taken the shots correctly, this is good news; if not, **practice makes perfect.**

Look at the Sequence

TEACHER: Soccer skills need to be taught in a set sequence, as a similar pattern of events will also take place in a top class game. Unless you point the sequence out, it is easily left unnoticed or forgotten. The most common sequence is when a player receives the ball ⇒ quickly controls it ⇒ lifts her head ⇒ decides on her action ⇒ then executes her play. Any sequence of events is important to learn as it will steady the pupil and help her to assess the play around her. So the older and quicker she gets, the more controlled her reactions will be.

LESSON 7
TERRIFIC REFLEX ACTIONS

TEACHER: Can you pass a ball over a short distance accurately? Face the pupil, 5–7 yards away from him and pass a fast ball along the ground to him. The pupil will need to watch the speed of the ball, then **bring his foot back to cushion the ball.** He must use **alternate feet** to trap the ball.

PUPIL: Keeping your eye on the ball, **lean forward and relax.** Bring your foot back at the moment of impact to cushion the speed of the ball and limit the bounce.

Speed Up the Control

TEACHER: Face the pupil, about 8–10 yards away from him. Tell him to turn to face the other way (fig. 46a). Now pass a fast ball towards the pupil, at the same time calling "turn." Limit the amount of time the pupil has to turn and trap the ball. Tell the pupil "head up" as he controls the ball. If he has difficulties, tell him to turn quicker, otherwise call "turn" sooner before the ball reaches him—this will give him more time to react.

PUPIL:
1. Quickly turn and control the ball, as in fig. 46b.
2. **Get your head up, look left then right.**
3. **Wait a few seconds.**
4. Now look back down to the ball.
5. Use the **inside** of your foot to pass back to the teacher, as in fig. 46c.

Fig. 46 a) Pupil has his back to the teacher and waits for the command "turn."
b) Pupil quickly turns to control the ball.
c) Pupil quickly lifts his head then looks left and right before passing the ball back to the teacher.

Make sure to follow this five-part sequence in order.

Fig. 47 Turning counterclockwise and clockwise.

Turn the Pupil Either Way

TEACHER: Still with the same exercise, this time, before you call "turn," tell the pupil whether he is to turn counter-clockwise or clockwise (fig. 47).

• Now tell the pupil which foot to trap the ball with before you give the command "turn."

• For teachers who find it difficult to pass the ball fast along the ground, throw or drop-kick the ball to the pupil. This could be a high (fig. 48) or low ball, but tell the pupil whhich foot to use to control the ball, and which way to turn before you deliver the ball.

Fig. 48   A higher ball, but still aimed towards the pupil's feet.

- **The most important factor is how the pupil reacts and gains control of the ball. He must move quickly, but relax when the ball nears him.**
These movements will help ball control and composure.

PUPIL: A ball in the air is harder to control than one along the ground, so this exercise will keep you on your toes. After turning, keep your eye on the ball $\Rightarrow$ move quickly $\Rightarrow$ then relax.

LESSON 8
ONE-ON-ONE PLAY

The next lesson requires coolness as well as agility and shows the need for players to think and steady their actions. **The younger the pupil the more strictly the rules must be adhered to.**

For this lesson you only need a small playing area, about 12 feet long by 10 feet wide. Make up goals 30 inches wide at either end of the "field." The first part of this lesson is devoted to attacking. Ten-minute practices are adequate.

TEACHER: Do not tackle the pupil. The pupil must feel confident against an opponent, so allow her 90% possession of the ball. Let her experiment with side moves, turning you one way then the other. Allow the pupil to go past you, but from her own initiative. Do not let the pupil shoot from a distance. Keep within this small area and, if you are unfit or as old as I am, take it easy and let her do most of the work! Remind the pupil, **"head up".**

PUPIL: This is a good opportunity for you to gain confidence on the ball. **Try at all times to move the ball into a space away from the teacher.** Sometimes roll the ball backward, but mainly move sideways, left, then right and so on, until a space has opened up for you to go forward. **Keep the ball away from the teacher using quick side-to-side movements,** moving one or two yards only. Make the most of this exercise; practice the following skills:

Fig. 49   Put the teacher off balance and pretend to strike the ball.

- Pretend that you are going to strike the ball, but stop
  your foot just before it reaches it. This feint may allow you
  to put the teacher off balance (fig. 49). Then push the ball
  behind him. Pretend to strike the ball with your left and
  then your right foot.
- With the ball at your feet, pretend you are going to run to
  the right or the left by taking a step in that direction. Put
  your shoulder down to make it look more convincing.
  Then take the ball the other way, as in fig. 50. Practice this
  either way and you will confuse the teacher.
- Place the ball in front of you and step one foot sideways
  over it. Now use the same foot to tap the ball sideways.
  The direction in which you step over the ball will
  determine whether you use the inside or outside of your
  foot to tap the ball. Practice this with your right and left
  feet. Use this trick combined with body movements and
  you will definitely confuse the teacher! (See fig. 51.)

Fig. 50   Confuse the teacher then take the ball the other way.

Fig. 51   Pupil steps over the ball and teacher leans the same way. Pupil takes the ball in the other direction. Keep your head up.

You must keep your head up and look to see if you are confusing the teacher. If not, make the pretense more convincing. Practice with alternate feet and let your body sway to emphasize the deception.

One-on-One Defending

TEACHER: We now have a slight variation from the previous exercise. Teacher, how good are you on the ball? You are now the attacker. Try to confuse the pupil with some tricks. You will need possession of the ball at least 50% of the time. Encourage the pupil **not to dive in and tackle you**—tell her to jockey you and **be patient.** The pupil must stay on her feet, keep on her toes, watch the ball, and wait for the right moment to tackle you. In the future, she is sure to come up against some skillful opponents, so this is good practice.

PUPIL: Practice defending in a one-on-one situation correctly. **Do not rush any tackles unless you are certain of winning the ball.** Mistakes look clumsy and can lose your team a game. The best way to keep a good attacker at bay or to win the ball is to **anticipate her movements.** Try to be patient, watching to see if the teacher makes an error. Turn at the same speed as he does, keeping about three feet away from him. Keep your eye on the ball.

More One-on-One Practice

TEACHER: You must practice one-on-one play regularly, but only in a 2–3 yard area. This will help to steady the pupil's ball control in tight situations.

Face the pupil, 1 yard away from her. Tell her to **move sideways with the ball,** left then right and so on (fig. 52). Follow the pupil's movements, but **do not tackle her**. You may, however, clip the ball from her feet every now and then. The pupil's movements must stay **within this 2–3 yard area.** Tell her to keep her head up, especially if she is young. As the pupil's ability increases, force her to work harder to keep the ball, but take it easy—don't wear yourself out!

Fig. 52   Keep your head up and move sideways with the ball.

PUPIL: Vary your movements to the left and to the right to try to put the teacher off balance. Look for an opportunity to push the ball past the teacher or through his legs (fig. 53). Stop every now and then and pretend that you are going to move to one side. Your teacher will follow you and he may open his legs just enough for you to push the ball between them. Keep your head up before and after any move.

TEACHER: Face the pupil and let her have possession of the ball. Move slowly towards the pupil in a brief attempt to take the ball. The pupil should roll the ball backward away from you, using the sole of her shoe. Then, at an opportune moment, she should take the ball either to the left or the right. The pupil must use **alternate feet to roll the ball backward** (fig. 54), but she can use either foot to tap the ball sideways.

PUPIL: With this exercise, roll the ball back only one yard, then take the ball sideways. Try to **speed up this action without losing control of the ball.**

Fig. 53 Look for an opportunity to push the ball through the teacher's legs. Keep your head up before and after any move.

Fig. 54 Use alternate feet to roll the ball backward.

LESSON 9
MORE CIRCLE MOVEMENTS

PUPIL: Do you remember the imaginary circle in lesson 3? Well, you are going to jog around it again. Your teacher will stand in the middle of the circle and throw or kick the ball to you. Keep your **head up** at all times, apart from when you are controlling or striking the ball.

TEACHER: Tell the pupil to jog **clockwise** around the imaginary circle. Call **"control"** and, at the same time, throw the ball overhand just in front of the pupil's feet (fig. 55). The pupil should control the ball ⇒ jog a few paces ⇒ then smoothly strike the ball back to you using his left foot.

Fig. 55 Teacher calls "control" and throws the ball in front of the pupil's feet. Pupil jogs clockwise, so he uses his left foot to receive the ball and pass it back.

Now tell the pupil to jog **counterclockwise,** so he uses his **right foot** to strike the ball back to you. You can give the command **"turn"** at any time. If you are able to kick an accurate ball, pass it along the ground to the pupil. Use this method at random moments.

- Still with the same exercise, tell the pupil to pass the ball back to you using the **inside** of his foot.
- Again with the same exercise, tell the pupil to control the ball ⇒ take it in small circles, clockwise or counterclockwise (as in lesson 3) ⇒ then pass or strike the ball back to you.

Tell the pupil what to do before he starts jogging, and make one change after each full circle.

Meeting the Ball

TEACHER: In soccer games, children often wait for the ball to arrive at their feet when it is passed to them, or they run forward when expecting to receive a pass from behind. While both actions occur frequently in top-level soccer, they may prove to be a hindrance to a young player. Lack of forethought or unnecessary forward runs will not help a young player make progress. With this in mind, practice meeting the ball regularly, so that the pupil learns how to meet a ball correctly from any direction.

LESSON 10
THROW-INS AND MEETING
THE BALL

We now see some throw-ins and meeting the ball. This lesson will combine ball control with game tactics, so increasing the pupil's need to really think about what is going on around him.

Fig. 56   Pupil jogs away from teacher and waits for the command "turn."

TEACHER: Hold the ball behind your head as if to take a throw-in towards the pupil. Now tell the pupil to turn and jog away from you (fig. 56), with his back to you. When you are ready, call **"turn."** The pupil should turn to face you, then jog toward you. Now choose a sensible moment to throw the ball toward the pupil's feet. He should meet the moving ball and make a first-time pass back to you. Vary the direction in which the pupil jogs: straight in front of you, to your left, and to your right. Throw the ball low toward the ground and limit the amount of bounce.

Now repeat the exercise, but this time ask the pupil to **sprint** toward you.

Note: You may find it difficult to throw the ball at the correct time for the pupil, or the ball may bounce awkwardly. If so, use the same exercise as above but pass the ball along the ground instead of throwing-in. This will serve as a good way of promoting a meeting with the ball.

Fig. 57   Pupil abruptly slows down and passes a first-time ball back to teacher.

PUPIL: Keep your eye on the ball. Pass a first-time ball back to the teacher using the most convenient foot. Always

slow down when you meet the ball so that you can pass accurately (fig. 57). When you have completed all of these variations you must **swap positions** with the teacher and practice a few throw-ins yourself. Throw the ball in toward the teacher sensibly—you don't need to knock him out!

More Throw-Ins

TEACHER: Use the same three directions and tell the pupil to turn and sprint toward you as before. Again, this will show the need for the pupil to steady his pace when meeting the ball.

a   b   c

Fig. 58   a) Trap the ball then pass back to teacher.
                b) Trap the ball then turn and dribble the ball away from teacher.
                c) Tap the ball to one side using your left and right feet.

Using these same throw-ins:
* Tell the pupil to **trap the ball,** then swiftly **make the pass** to you, as in fig. 58a.
* Tell the pupil to **trap the ball,** then turn and **dribble it away** from you, as in fig. 58b.

- Tell the pupil to **tap the moving ball gently to one side** using the inside of his foot, as in fig. 58c. He should practice using either foot, so he taps the ball left or right, then tell him to run a few yards with it.

Note: Again, these throws will be difficult to perfect so try passing the ball along the ground as well.

Throw-Ins to the Chest and Forehead

TEACHER: We'll now try a throw for the more advanced pupil. This must be taken with the pupil fairly close to you. Throw the ball gently onto the pupil's chest, and he should use his chest firmly to direct the ball back to your feet, as in fig. 59a. (For the younger pupils, "chesting" the ball is in the next lesson.)

Fig. 59   a) Firmly chest the ball back to teacher.
           b) A positive header back to teacher.

Now take some throw-ins directly onto the pupil's forehead. Tell him to head the ball back to your feet (fig. 59b). Are you getting fed up with throwing the ball yet?

The Longer Throw-In

It is now the pupil's turn to practice throwing some throw-ins. It is important for the pupil to master a longer throw, as one day he may find himself in a situation where this type of throw is needed.

PUPIL: You may now practice some longer throw-ins, but do not use this type of throw if you want the ball to be passed back to you!

Hold the ball correctly to get a feel for the action.

- Spread your fingers to the side of and behind the ball, your thumbs at the bottom pointing towards each other.
- Bring the ball up behind your head and, at the same time, bend your knees as in fig. 60a.
- You should feel the tension in your wrists as your fingers are level behind you. If not, twist your wrists back toward the ground.

    a   b   c

Fig. 60   a) Twist wrists to get a feel for the direction. Bend knees and bring elbows slightly forward.

              b) Thrust the ball up and forward.

              c) Walking forward with the ball, bring feet together and then thrust the ball.

- Holding this position, bend your knees and keep your elbows slightly forward. You should now feel you can throw the ball up in the air.

The thrust.

- Practice slowly to start with, so that you get a good feel for this action, but the faster you can propel the ball from your hands, the further it will travel.
- Starting from a standstill, twist your wrist and rock the ball back and forth, as if to throw the ball. This will give you a sense of direction.
- Now bend your knees and thrust the ball up and forward using a fast action from your arms. The upward and forward movement should leave you with your hands in the air, like the child in fig. 60b.
- Now try doing the same action while walking forward. As you are about to throw the ball, bring your feet together and thrust the ball, as in fig. 60c.

LESSON 11

OTHER THROW-IN EXERCISES

This lesson is useful for enhancing ball control, and it allows a bit of fun in the process!

Trapping a High or Low Ball onto your Chest

TEACHER: Stand facing the pupil, a few yards away from her. Throw the ball onto the ground so it bounces toward the pupil in the air. You can judge the speed of the ball from the bounce, and make the ball go either low or high in the air. Take care how you direct the ball if your pupil is young.

PUPIL: When the ball is coming at you, lean back and cushion the ball with your chest, as in fig. 61a.

To trap a low ball with your chest, lean forward when the ball is upon you, arch your shoulders and then direct the ball to the ground, as in fig. 61b.

More Ways to Control the Ball

TEACHER: Face the pupil and either bounce the ball onto the ground, or throw the ball in the air. As the ball comes down, the pupil should cushion the ball using the lace area of her shoe. This will only be effective if she raises her foot under the ball and then brings it down at the same speed as the ball, as in fig. 62a. Practice using alternate feet.

Now bounce the ball so the pupil cushions the ball using her thighs, as in fig. 62b. As soon as the ball hits the pupil's

Fig. 61   a) Pupil leans back to cushion a high ball.
         b) Pupil leans forward to cushion a low ball.

thigh, tell her to straighten her leg. The ball will then drop to the ground near to the pupil's feet (fig. 62c).

Heading a Fast-Moving Ball
TEACHER: Throw the ball overhand for the pupil to head (fig. 63a). Start by throwing the ball gently, then increase the speed of the ball up to a reasonable testing pace. See how well

Fig. 62 a) Pupil lowers his foot to cushion the ball.
b) Pupil raises his thigh to meet the ball.
c) Pupil straightens his leg and the ball drops to the ground.

the pupil copes, but be careful not to discourage her by pushing her too far. Move closer to the pupil so her reactions become quicker. This practice could take place with the pupil heading the ball onto a wall or high into the air. Refer back to the instructions for headers in lesson 4, page 28–32. Do not try this exercise if the pupil is young. Older pupils need only practice this minimally.

PUPIL: You need to keep your eye on the ball and meet the ball with your forehead (fig. 63b). Your forehead should always end up facing the direction in which you want the ball to go.

Fig. 63 a) Throwing a fast ball.
b) The center of the forehead directs the ball.

LESSON 12

SPECIAL WAYS OF STRIKING THE BALL

One quality of a great player is the ability to strike the ball using either foot, making the ball go where they want it to go, how they want it to go: high, low, long, swerving, or fast. Sounds difficult? Well, even some top players struggle to use either foot and do not always play the ball that accurately. Therefore, to be able to strike the ball low using either foot is a good start for any youngster.

Some Facts on Lifting the Ball

We are often told that, in order to lift the ball off the ground, we must lean back. Well, this is not necessary and may confuse your actions. Leaning back will occur naturally, just after you strike the ball. To prove the point, stand upright and bring your kicking leg all the way back, then forward in one big sweep, as if to strike the ball. In this movement your body will follow a natural course: you will first lean forward (fig. 64a) and then backward (fig. 64b).

We can either limit or emphasize our body movements in order to control a shot. For example, we lean over the ball to keep a shot low and we stand upright, then force ourselves back, to lift the ball high. However, this does not always mean that the ball will travel where we want it to go. How our foot makes contact with the ball is the deciding factor for the ball's direction of travel.

Fig. 64 Bring the kicking leg back and forth—see how your body leans.
a) Leg back—you lean forward.
b) Leg forward—you lean back.

PUPIL: Try exaggerating the way the ball is lifted. Bring your leg back and bend your knee so that your foot is behind you and almost parallel to the ground, as in fig. 65a. Now use a sweeping action to strike the ball, turning your heel inward and directing your foot well under the ball so your foot comes closer to the ground and hits the lower part of the ball (fig. 65b).

Practice this from a standstill, and then by walking up to the ball first. See if you can make the ball travel straight and rise high off the ground. If you keep your eye on the ball and make the correct contact you should chip the ball well off the ground. Still use the lace area of your shoe and practice alternating your feet.

TEACHER: Stand alongside the pupil. Make sure that the action is correct, then get him to chip the ball to you.

Striking with Power

TEACHER: We will now shift the emphasis to encouraging a strike with power. Note that trying to hit the ball in this

Fig. 65   a) Bring foot back almost parallel to the ground—heel inward.
          b) Direct your foot well under the ball.

manner is not a good idea for youngsters as, for them, accuracy is more important.

PUPIL: This is different from the last exercise in that you do not need to achieve lift. You may use power in conjunction with any method of striking the ball. But remember—how your foot makes contact with the ball will determine in which direction the ball travels.

- To strike the ball low with power, keep your eye on the middle part of the ball but focus more on your foot gaining speed as it makes contact with the ball (fig. 66a). Really smack the ball hard. Your foot should follow through, waist high, with your leg ending up straight, as in fig. 66b. We sometimes see a player striking the ball so hard that both feet come off the ground as the force of the follow-through has momentarily lifted his body off the ground!

Fig. 66   a) Focus more on your foot gaining speed.
b) Follow through fast. Your leg should end up straight.

Fig. 67   Rapidly increase the speed of your foot. Make sure the ball travels straight and fast.

- You will only get power behind the ball when you force an impact. You will not be able to force any impact on the ball unless the speed of your foot rapidly increases. To explain this further: bring your leg back, then slowly forward, but rapidly increase the speed of your foot as it lowers toward the ball. This acceleration will create a strong impact. Practice this method from a standstill, to get a feel for the action. You can emphasize your body movement by leaning forward to keep the ball low. Strike with your foot at the middle part of the ball, and make sure the ball travels quite fast and straight (fig. 67).

Fig. 68   If your body is relaxed you will naturally lean back. The ball leaves your foot fast from a good foot contact.

- Now step a few paces up to the ball and, using a more continuous leg action, really smack the ball hard, following through with your leg swiftly. This action will cause you to lean back, as in fig. 68, so make sure you have a good foot contact to produce the correct effect. You must keep your **eye on the ball.**

The Long Ball with Lift

PUPIL: The way to gain lift and distance from the ball is to strike your foot just below the middle of the ball and use some power.

We have practiced chipping the ball to achieve a high lift previously (pages 68–69). If your foot strikes just below the middle of the ball this will lift the ball, but less high up. If you add power, the ball will rise steadily and the lift will increase.

Fig. 69   Fix your eyes just below the middle of the ball. This will make it easier to hit the ball correctly.

Jog up to the ball from only a few paces away and fix your eyes just below the middle of the ball (fig. 69). Where you place your nonstriking foot will make a big difference. If it is too far forward this may reduce your power and thus the lifting effect. If your foot is placed too far behind the ball you will need to stretch to reach it, in which case again you may reduce your power, or even fall. For the best strike, place your nonstriking foot alongside the ball, and powerfully strike the ball off the ground (fig. 70).

TEACHER: Whacking the ball to gain power and lift is **not** a good idea to practice too often, especially if the child is

Fig. 70   Use some power—the ball will travel and rise steadily off the
ground.

young. For him to know what to do with the ball and produce
some effect is adequate.

Curling the Ball

TEACHER: Using the lace area of the shoe provides many
options. The player can curl the ball either left or right, and
may use this action with lift or power. However, if a child is

young, it is better not to attempt these variations too soon, as this may disrupt what he has previously learned or may become boring. Just striking the ball straight, using either foot, is sufficient for youngsters.

a

b

Fig. 71   a) Follow your foot through and around in front of you.
b) Strike the ball using the inner part of your shoe.

PUPIL: To make the ball curl inward, strike the ball using the **inner** part of your shoe, near the lace holes (fig. 71b). Practice by first standing alongside the ball so you get a feel for the action. Aim your foot **just below the middle part of the ball** and follow your foot through (fig. 71a). Practice using alternate feet.

Now jog up to the ball and, approaching the ball more from the side, use some power (fig. 72).

To curl the ball outward, strike the ball using the **outer** part of your foot near the lace holes (fig. 73c). As before, follow

Fig. 72 Approach the ball more from the side. Jog up to the ball and use some power.

your foot through as you strike (fig. 73b). This type of strike will not produce any effect unless the ball travels low, with power, and ends up right on target. This strike can look like a poor kick if it's not really accurate, but it is worth practicing with either foot. Try the approach in fig. 73a opposite.

Using the Top and Outer Part of your Foot

PUPIL: Stand with your feet 6 inches apart. Turn your right foot inward, and kick the ball forward using the top and outer part of your foot, as in fig. 74a. You will perhaps feel awkward performing this type of kick, but practice using either foot. You will eventually get a feel for the movement and will be able to hit the ball with some power, following your foot through (fig. 74b). This type of kick is useful to pass or direct the ball quickly in certain situations.

TEACHER: This method of kicking the ball is a different technique from what has already been learned, so be sure to keep it separate from other exercises.

Fig. 73 a) A typical approach using the right foot.
b) Follow through with your foot.
c) Use the outer part of your shoe.

Fig. 74   a) Use either foot and build up to hitting the ball with power.
b) Use the top and outer part of your shoe.

Juggling with the Ball

PUPIL: This is an exercise you may know already. Juggling with the ball will help your balance and ball control, yet it is only seen as pregame flair. This is quite difficult to do with both feet, let alone with your head, thighs, shoulders, arms, and back. Juggling may take some time to master, but it is worth practicing. However, you don't juggle with the ball during a game, so if you do not become an expert, so what?

Use the sole of your shoe to pull the ball backward (fig. 75a), then flick it up in the air using the lace area of your shoe. Try to keep the ball a short distance from the ground and flick the ball toward you. Now use alternate feet to keep it up in the air (fig. 75b). You could try:

Fig. 75 a) Roll the ball backward.
b) Flick the ball up a short distance from the ground. Use alternate feet.

- keeping the ball up in the air using the top of your thighs or forehead (fig. 76)
- juggling the ball from one part of your body to another
- or walking forward while keeping the ball up in the air.

These are not very easy, so try juggling only for short periods of time. Then, if you are really good, get ready for the circus!

While on the subject of showing off your moves, try this useful back pass. Walk away from the teacher with the ball and then use your heel to jab the ball back. Use alternate feet.

Side Foot Practice

TEACHER: Remember lesson 1, where you threw the ball to the pupil and he would gently strike it back to you? This exercise is similar, except the pupil uses the side of his foot to pass the ball back into your arms.

Fig. 76   You could keep the ball in the air using your forehead.

Fig. 77   Pupil uses the side of his foot to pass the ball into the teacher's arms.

Start by bouncing the ball in front of him and then move on to throwing the ball directly onto his foot. The pupil should use alternate feet to side-foot the ball back to you, as in fig. 77.

LESSON 13
MOVE AND SHOOT

This next lesson will bring your skills into play, but will also show you the need for poise. A change of pace from quick to slow is extremely important in soccer. With these exercises, try to use a soccer field and a goal.

TEACHER: The pupil will strike the ball from four different positions: left of the goal, either side of center, and right of the goal. Your job is to be the goalkeeper, or to stand behind the goal to collect any missed balls. Tell the pupil to dribble fast, but make sure he **changes his pace** and **prepares himself** before striking the ball. Composure and accuracy are vital, not power.

PUPIL: Stand outside the penalty area and dribble the ball fast toward the goal (fig. 78a). **Keep your head up.** As you approach the goal, **abruptly slow down** and take your time with the shot. Tap the ball forward but very slightly to one side as you are about to shoot (fig. 78b). It is more effective to position the ball correctly first than to move sideways to strike the ball. Hit the **middle part** of the ball to keep it low. Use your right foot to strike the ball, as in fig. 78c.

- Follow the same sequence from the four different positions shown in fig. 79.
- Now execute the four shots from the four positions, but this time use your **left foot.** You weren't trying to get away without doing that, were you?

Fig. 78 a) Dribble ball fast toward the goal . . .
b) . . . abruptly slow down and tap ball slightly diagonally . . .
c) . . . strike the middle of the ball.

Fig. 79 Strike from four different positions.

Speed up the Control and Take Time with the Shot

The importance of a change is now demonstrated again in a new exercise, still in the goal area. This further highlights the need for composure and for the pupil to tap the ball forward before striking. This exercise is **not** a model for how to score at close range, but features controlled striking.

Fig. 80 Teacher kicks a high ball.

TEACHER: Stand in the goal and ask the pupil to stand beyond the penalty spot. Throw or kick a high ball to the pupil, as in fig. 80. The pupil **must** follow the sequence below and do it with alternate feet: first the left foot to control and strike the ball, next time the right foot to control and strike the ball. After all, we don't want things too easy for her! While the pupil is having fun she also needs a good test.

PUPIL: Move quickly and control the ball ⇒ look up (fig. 81) ⇒ tap the ball forward and perhaps slightly to one side (only a touch, otherwise you may lose valuable time chasing after it, fig. 82) ⇒ strike the ball (fig. 83).

Speed Up the Control but Maintain the Composure
TEACHER: To further reinforce the techniques learned in the previous exercise, tell the pupil to turn and face the other way (fig. 84) then throw or kick the ball. Give the command

Fig. 81   Pupil moves quickly ⇒ controls ball ⇒ lifts head up.

Fig. 82   Pupil taps the ball slightly forward.

Fig. 83   Pupil strikes ball at goal.

"turn." The pupil needs to quickly turn ⇒ control the ball ⇒ lift up her head ⇒ tap the ball forward ⇒ then execute the strike. **Make sure the pupil follows this sequence.**

Fig. 84   The pupil turns his back to the teacher and follows the sequence

- Now vary the height and speed of the ball. Make the pupil work to control the ball.
- Now tell the pupil to stand well to the side of the goal and do the same (fig. 85). This position will narrow his shooting angle, and remind the pupil of the importance of **lifting her head.** In a game, another member of the team might be in a good scoring position, so a side pass may be better!

Fig. 85   The pupil stands well to the side of the goal and receives the ball, lifting his head to see whether a cross or a pass is an option.

LESSON 14
THE RETURN BALL

This next lesson is again in the goal area (or against a wall with a small target area), but with passing moves this time. This will give another insight into making first time passes and the importance of playing the ball in the direction you are facing. These moves may seem quite basic, but do not underestimate their value. This type of play can arise in many situations all over the field.

Fig. 86   Teacher passes and pupil meets the ball.

TEACHER: Look at fig. 86. Stand beyond the penalty spot and face the goal. Position the pupil, facing you, near the goalpost to your left. Throw or kick a low, bouncing ball toward the pupil, then move a few paces forward. The pupil should run to meet the ball, then pass it back, using her right foot, so you can shoot with your left foot. Only shoot if you want to. Now make it easier and pass the ball to the pupil along the ground. Alternate between a bouncing ball and a pass along the ground.

Fig. 87 Pupil passes the ball using right foot. Teacher uses left foot to shoot at the target.

PUPIL: As the teacher passes the ball to you, get off the mark and meet the ball. Using the inside of your right foot, pass the ball, directing it to just in front of the teacher's left foot, so that she can shoot if she wishes (fig. 87). This return pass shows how easily one of your teammates could score if your back is to the goal.

TEACHER: Now tell the pupil to stand in front of the other goalpost and repeat the exercise. This time the pupil will use her left foot to pass the ball back to you. You can then use your right foot to shoot at the goal. Only shoot if you want to: remember—you are the teacher!

Variations with the Return Ball

TEACHER: Tell the pupil to stand in the center of the goal area. Again, pass the ball to the pupil who should now meet the ball and play it back to you three separate ways: to your left, to your right, or straight back toward you. Remember that you do not have to shoot.

Now swap positions (fig. 88) and choose which way to play the ball back to the pupil (fig. 89). As the pupil is about to strike, move out of the way to make it easier for her to score, as in fig. 90. With a return ball, the pupil must use her most convenient foot to shoot, regardless of where the ball comes from. The pupil will most likely strike the ball contrary to the rule in lesson 6 (page 38). This does not matter, as long as she strikes the ball correctly and scores goals.

Fig. 88   The center of the goal is now used. Pupil passes to the teacher.

Fig. 89   Teacher chooses which way to pass the ball back to the pupil: left, right, or straight back.

Fig. 90   Teacher decides to pass the ball straight back to the pupil and gets out of the way. Pupil shoots at the goal.

PUPIL: You can practice first-time passes anywhere on the field. Pass the ball back and forth to the teacher, using the inside of your foot. It is very important to practice using either foot—otherwise, how do you learn to use both feet equally well in a game?

Vary your positions; move from side to side or jog up and down the field together. When possible, practice on a soccer field to get a feel for the space available in this whole area.

LESSON 15
ON THE FIELD

Playing a Ball Out of Defense

This next exercise will demonstrate safe play. During a game, a defender may need to play a long ball out of the danger area, or down the sidelines. A long ball must only be used if there is no option of making a short pass.

TEACHER: By now the pupil should be able to strike a ball reasonably well using either foot, so executing a long and accurate pass will eventually come quite easily to her. However, depending on her age, the ball may not travel as far as she would like. This is not very important as she will be stronger when she is older.

Position the pupil close to the center of the goal and stand on the right hand corner of the eighteen-yard box. Now kick the ball firmly to the pupil, in the air or along the ground. The pupil should trap the ball ⇒ take it left out of the danger area (in the direction you are standing) ⇒ then strike the ball high toward you but over your head, using her left foot, as in fig. 91.

PUPIL: You must quickly control the ball ⇒ look up and, at the same time, take the ball away from the center of the goal ⇒ then deliver a long, high ball toward the teacher. Always approach the ball correctly and keep your eye on the ball when executing the strike. You do not need to run fast at the ball to gain power—your aim is to lift the ball and make it rise over the teacher's head.

Fig. 91   Pupil takes the ball out of the danger area and strikes a high ball over the teacher's head, using his left foot.

TEACHER: Now stand on the left-hand corner of the eighteen-yard box which is on your left, and repeat the exercise. The pupil should take the ball to his right-hand side and use his right foot to strike the ball. Practice three times on the right-hand side, three on the left-hand side. After kicking the ball to the pupil you can move further away, the distance depending on his age. Tell the pupil to keep trying to lift the ball over your head.

Awareness in Midfield

TEACHER: Position the pupil in the middle of the field, on the halfway line. Stand outside the circle and throw or kick the ball to her, as in fig. 92, then immediately jog in another direction. The pupil should control the ball, then either strike or pass the ball back to you. Before you start the exercise tell the pupil:
1. which foot to use to control the ball,
2. whether to strike or pass back, and which foot to use.
E.g. "Left foot control—right foot pass back" or "right foot control—right foot strike back."

The pupil should remain in the circle, but now you must vary the positions you throw or kick the ball from. Use at least four positions to allow the pupil to see the whole field and the different directions in which she will face during a game.

PUPIL: Control the ball and imagine that an opposing player is close by. Look up and quickly move the ball into a good

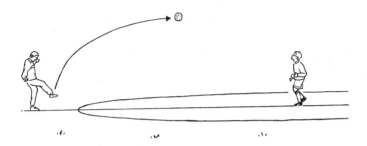

Fig. 92   Teacher kicks the ball to the pupil, then jogs to another position.

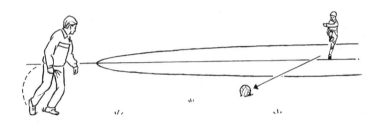

Fig. 93   Pupil controls the ball, then strikes it back to the teacher.

spot so you can execute a firm pass or strike accurately back to the teacher. Remember—it is easier for one of your own players to control the ball from a low, firm pass rather than one flying up in the air.

Corners

PUPIL: You will now practice taking some corners while the teacher stands near the penalty spot. You will again strike your foot against the lower part of the ball and make it curl in. Strike the ball using the inner part of your shoe near the lace holes. Take the corners from one side of the field, but strike the ball using alternate feet. The ball will either go slightly towards the goal or slightly away from the goal, depending on which foot you use (see figs. 94 and 95). If you have followed the course you should be able to take corners using either foot. Whether you do so in a game is another matter. This will depend on how much you perfect this, as well as your age and ability.

Fig. 94   **Right** foot curls ball **toward** goal.

Fig. 95   **Left** foot curls ball **away** from goal.

Now strike the ball using the center of the lace area of your shoe. Do you see the difference? While practicing, remain on one side of the field and, if necessary, reduce the distance between you and the goal. Try to perfect your corners by making correct contact with the ball. Only stand a couple of yards behind the ball before you strike it. You do not need to make a long run. When curling the ball, approach it more from the side.

Crossing the Ball

PUPIL: This is a similar action to that involved in taking corners, but this time you and the ball may be moving. This exercise is not a model for crossing the ball but, if practiced well, it will provide you with plenty of scope for variation.

Ask the teacher to stand on the penalty spot—he is your target man. Move quickly with the ball, up and down the sideline. Turn at least three times, as in fig. 96a. You must keep the ball under control, but also keep your head up so that you can see the goal (fig. 96b). Now cross the ball, aiming for the target man.

Now repeat the exercise; but this time, just before you turn, pretend to kick the ball with either foot. This will serve three important purposes:
1. to confuse your opponent
2. to let you decide which foot to use, and
3. to give you time to pick the best moment to cross the ball.
This trick makes it easier for you to get the ball past your opponent and into the goal area (fig. 96c).

Now try two more variations on the cross:
• strike the ball using the center of the lace area of your shoe
• curl the ball using the method described in lesson 12, page 74.
With each method, you will need to adjust your speed and turn your body accordingly. Use **alternate feet** to cross the ball and move gradually closer to the goal, depending on your age.

TEACHER: It is important that the pupil learns how to cross the ball using either foot. Bringing the pupil closer to you will

Fig. 96 a) Keeping your head up, move the ball quickly up and down the
sideline, turning at least three times before you cross the ball.
b) Look at the goal and at the teacher.
c) This time, the cross goes in.

make it easier for her to do this and so will improve her confidence.

Final Lesson! Tap in Some Goals

Now we have reached the end of the lessons—WELL DONE! Both teacher and pupil deserve a big round of applause for working so hard (or not so hard, as the case may be!). For a bit of fun to celebrate your achievements, let's see if teacher and pupil can score some easy goals.

Fig. 97   Pupil passes ball from the left so that the teacher taps in the goals with his left foot.

PUPIL: Position yourself as in fig. 97. Pass an accurate ball across the face of the goal, so the teacher can try to score some goals. Pass the ball from either side of the goal using your right foot, then your left foot, and so on. Strike the ball, and use a side-foot pass. Ask the teacher to try and tap the ball in using the inside of his foot. When you pass the ball from the right, the teacher should use his right foot to tap in the goals, and vice versa.

Fig. 98   Now swap positions – the teacher passes ball from the right so the pupil taps in the goals with his right foot.

TEACHER: Now swap positions and pass the ball from either side of the pupil, as in fig. 98. The pupil should then tap the ball into the goal using the inside of either foot.

To make it a bit more tricky, use a smaller goal, a set target, or even a goalkeeper. However you do it, both of you should keep your eyes on the ball, and do not miss!

ALL-AROUND VARIATIONS

PUPIL: This next section lists a number of points you can refer to, but, as your ability increases, most of these will become second nature to you.

Passing or Striking the Ball

Place one foot alongside the ball and keep your eye on the ball.
- *To increase height*, strike your foot at the lower part of the ball, close to the ground.
- *To keep the ball low*, strike your foot at the **middle** or **upper** part of the ball.
- *To curl a ball inward*, use the area between the lace area and the **inside** of your shoe to strike the ball.
- *To curl a ball outward*, use the area between the lace area and the **outside** of your shoe to strike the ball.
- *To increase power*, **speed up** your foot movement, then follow through, striking the ball accurately.
- *To increase the effect*, **accentuate** the body action and use more physical effort.

Controlling the Ball

Keep your eye on the ball, judge the speed the ball is traveling, and then cushion the bounce.
- *To control the ball with your feet*, use the **side** of your foot where possible.
- *To control a high ball with your chest*, **lean back** and cushion the ball with your chest.
- *To control a lower ball with your chest*, **lean forward**, arch your shoulders in, and direct the ball to the ground.

Heading the Ball

Keep your eyes open and direct the ball where you want it to go with your forehead. Your forehead should end up facing the same direction as the ball is traveling.

- *To head a fast-moving ball,* meet it with full **forehead contact.**
- *To head a slow-moving ball,* arch your back, bring your **neck back,** and **attack the ball.**
- *To make a glancing header,* make **slight forehead contact** with the ball.

THE FINAL PART

PRACTICE

PUPIL: We now arrive at the last section of the book, but, before we continue, let me remind you to **keep practicing all of the lessons.** Go over any areas where you feel there is a weakness. It is quite usual for a player to kick the ball with his best foot, or to rely on his strengths in a game. But if you have any weaknesses these will always show. Choose from all the lessons and use a good variety of exercises each time you practice. This should help you to learn more quickly and it will make it more interesting.

The first part of this section will give some advice to the very young and to those of you who have not yet started playing for a team. Do not rush into playing for a team; consider how proficient you could become if you practice your skills for just two hours each week. This would give you loads of ball possession in a year; in a game you only get about three minutes.

Why Practice?
Most players will need about three months' regular practice to see any real improvement in their skills, or even longer if they are playing for a team. Remember, if you are lacking the skills in practice, how are you going to cope at a faster pace when playing in a team?

What Position?
If you have practiced over several months, you should be fairly confident playing any position on the field. The more skill you have acquired, the more adaptable you will be. You

could end up playing in only one position, although I feel that this is not a good idea. You will, at some point, find the position which best suits you.

Limit Your Speed

It is very important not to rush your play. Take your time and use the skills that you have learned. Limit the use of speed when in possession of the ball and try, when possible, to keep hold of the ball. This is not a suggestion that you slouch around the soccer field, nor that you hog the ball, but merely a way to avoid making mistakes, while at the same time improving your confidence on the ball.

Hold on to the Ball

If you proceed slowly with the ball, and do not always run forward, you will become more aware of the other players around you. As you become older and gain more experience, you will know where to play the ball even before you receive it. More passing options will become available to you, your speed will increase on the field and will be used more often, though with some restraint. This will be a natural progression as you grow, and as you play more games.

The Wrong Time

We often see older teenage players who have skill but fail to make an impression on the field. Often their eagerness causes them to make blatant mistakes. This can occur when poor team play or hurrying forces them into bad habits. An example of this is the youngster who just happens to be a fast runner. He can use his speed in preference to skill which sometimes looks impressive. However, he has probably learned to use his speed at the wrong time and so neglected his technique. This may prove to be his downfall.

Lacking Speed

A player may be skillful throughout his childhood but, when he gets older, find that he lacks speed. We should never presume everything will work out just as we hope. It is better to take your time when you are young than rush your play and become susceptible to bad habits. A player will always shine by making use of his skill with the ball as his main asset.

THE LEVELS OF SOCCER

Young Success
A child of eight or nine has a long way to go before she reaches adult-level soccer. Some youngsters may be noticed by national soccer clubs. This is no guarantee of success, but it's nonetheless encouraging.

Will I Get Noticed?
Youngsters between the ages of twelve and sixteen have a good opportunity to show their abilities. Schools will field players to represent their town or county. Clubs will nominate players to represent leagues. This, together with playing in a good team or reaching a cup final, may lead to some recognition. However, there is no set route to success. Opportunities may come and go in soccer, but there are other ways to get recognized and progress. Throughout the country there are different levels of soccer, from the lower adult ranks through to the National Leagues. Many a player has come from the lower ranks and made it to top-class soccer. Playing at the local senior level may prove to be a good start for any youngster.

How to Play when you are Older
Watch the top players in action, whether live or on TV, and you will see that they are agile, accurate, quick, and they make the game look easy. Well, playing the game is easy to them. The only trial they face is a training session between games. So, if you are sixteen or older, what should you be doing? Copying the best player you know of and following her pattern of play.

The Test
If you learn to play soccer steadily at first, you will progress over the years and use more speed, more so when really put to the test. All players will face a test when they try to reach a

higher level of soccer. You will need to prove that you are capable of fitting in with the team, first by showing adequate skill and composure, then by speeding up your pace. Each level is that much harder to reach than the last, yet your skill and composure will remain the real test. If you are also quick and agile you may go higher—even to the top!

The Way to Play
Observe any children's game and see if you can spot the best player in that team. If you are not sure, ask their manager. Observe what this player does in the game. I am sure you will recognize how she reacts on the ball. She will be agile, yet stay firmly on the ball. She will keep her poise, move in any direction, and show confidence, with only short bursts of speed. She will not chase around needlessly.

Save Your Energy
Many younger children's soccer games are quite physical, yet are often lacking in skill. Depending on the quality of the team, you will need to adjust to this and, to some extent, play your own game. This is not to say that you must pussyfoot around, but only use your strength when you need to.

THE IMPORTANCE OF GOOD TEACHING

TEACHER: The **way** the pupil is taught is just as important as **what** he is taught, so it is vital that you get it right at this early stage in your youngster's learning. Here are some points to consider.

Ball Contact
Correct ball contact is a vital skill so should be the first thing to learn. In soccer, as in all ball sports, making a good contact with the ball comes with experience. However, compared to a golf ball or a tennis ball, a soccer ball is quite large, so this should make it easier to strike it accurately. The biggest problem can occur when the ball is traveling fast and low toward the player—this really puts his judgment to the test.

Striking a fast moving ball low and accurately is not easy, but if he is going to shoot in this situation, it is preferable to miss the target wide than to sweep the ball high into the air. The pupil should practice low shots and direct the ball so it travels close to the ground. The important points to remember are for him to:

- keep his eye on the ball
- strike the ball correctly.

Accuracy

A player's accuracy on the field is fundamental to his and his team's performance. There is no point in shooting, heading, or passing the ball, unless it goes exactly in the direction that it is supposed to. All players make mistakes on the field, but when practicing there is no need to rush. This also applies in warm-up, or when just tapping the ball between two or three players. The pupil needs to perfect his aim and learn to slow his pace.

Increasing the Pupil's Awareness

A player must learn to keep his head up and look around him. If he keeps his eye fixed only on the ball, another player may then sweep in and take it away from him. This could happen if the ball is coming toward him, or even just as he receives it. A player should only look at the ball as it nears him. It only takes a short time to pass or control a ball, but he needs a long look to see who's around . . .

Keep it Simple

There is no need for youngsters to exert too strenuous an effort. Most young players will gain more from practicing simple skills such as quick ball control, agile movements, and kicking the ball around than from grueling sessions of repeated long kicks.

Changes that Occur

When playing a game of soccer, changes will occur in the way a player executes a skill. Such changes are governed by several factors:

- the speed of a pass
- the condition of the field
- how much time the player has on the ball
- the player's own peculiarities and so on.

Players will change their technique to suit a situation, so set patterns are bound to be disrupted during the course of a game, regardless of how they have been executed in practice.

Motivation

When a child is enjoying being taught, he learns more. His interest will be maintained if you vary the sequence of his exercises. As he progresses, praise him and explain the reason for the praise. Watch his performance closely and do not scold him if he makes a mistake: instead, suggest a way in which to correct the error. At times you will need to compromise, especially when things are not going quite as well as they should be. Be prepared to pause the practice if he is becoming distracted or irritable. Let the child do something different with the ball, or allow him to choose what he wants to do (within reason!).

Feedback

Using the one-on-one teaching method will make it easier for the pupil to improve his performance. Look for any exercises that may seem difficult, then, if you feel you are up to it, demonstrate the sequence to the pupil—but be careful to get it right! Alternatively, watch a professional soccer game and point out the skills that the pupil needs to practice. When he performs a technique correctly, ask him to describe how the action felt so that he develops an understanding for the correct movement and will be able to repeat it.

Fitness and Fatigue

Most children are reasonably fit, so they should be able to perform a suitable amount of ball work without becoming too tired. However, putting a child under too much strain will not increase a youngster's skill. Therefore, do not increase a child's physical work until he shows good progress in his skills.

The Way we are Built

Players vary in shapes and sizes: tall, short, thin, or stocky. But size doesn't matter. All soccer players need to be very fit and have a high level of stamina, but even this will vary from one player to the next. Youngsters are all different and all will show strengths in a variety of ways. Do not attempt to anticipate a child's development or chances of success from his present build or stature.

Expectations

We all set high expectations at one time or another, but these can prove damaging, not only to a teacher, but also to a child. It is easy to think only of success, but a youngster will do better if not put under pressure to succeed. There will be proud moments when a child does progress, and disappointment if he fails. However, "pushiness" and impatience will not improve a child's ability or performance. All a teacher can do is encourage, support, and praise the child, hoping that he will try to do the best that he possibly can.

An Adult's Influence

The influence that a parent, tutor, or other guiding adult has over a child may be greater than you think. Now and again, one sees parents of very young children shouting aggressive abuse from the sidelines. Children often react to this aggression by running faster, making more mistakes, tackling badly, or even causing fouls. Adults **must** learn to keep their emotions under control. This behavior will never help a child to progress, and may even spoil his chances.

To call out "well done—great pass!" or "great shot!" or "never mind, get your head up!" shows a far more positive attitude. Your enthusiasm should encourage *good play,* rather than simply winning.

Other ways to influence a child beneficially are to tell him to "keep your head up," "take your time," "control the ball," or "don't rush your pass," and so on. You must stay calm throughout the game and let the youngster get on with playing. Brief and basic advice is enough, given just before the game or perhaps at halftime.

THE GAME TO PRACTICE

TEACHER: How do we make a youngster more aware of what's going on around him in a game? How do we increase his confidence and encourage him to pass more? The answer: restrict the player going forward on the ball and limit tackles in a game.

Young players have an urge to go forward, especially when they shouldn't. This is evident when a player runs headlong into trouble, or when she misses a good opportunity to pass. Holding up the play will make youngsters more aware of the other players around them. This will create more backup play and passing around the team, instead of their teammates scattering in all directions.

The following game is designed purely to help increase all players' levels of awareness by holding up play in an exaggerated way. You can play the game with any even number of players between four and twenty. Use a field relative in size to the number of players.

The game is played just like any other game, with the following extra rules:

1. The player who has possession of the ball **cannot go forward with the ball.** She may take the ball sideways, backward, or pass the ball in any direction, but she must not run or even walk forward more than one or two steps with the ball.

2. When a player has possession of the ball, all opposing players **must stay a distance of one yard away** and **not tackle.** Any loose balls will go in the opposition's favor, more so if there is a dispute. Any 50-50 balls will go in favor of the first player to put her foot on top of the ball. The opposing player must then back off to the one-yard distance.

3. No long shots are allowed. If you have a total of four players in the game, a player must be within two yards of the goal before she can shoot. If you have a total of six players in the game, a player must be within three yards of the goal to shoot. Increase the shooting distance by one yard for each additional two players. Therefore, with twenty

players the shots at goal will be no further than ten yards away.
4.   Free kicks will be awarded against any player not adhering to these rules. All other soccer rules will apply as normal.
Use these rules then go back to your normal game and spot the difference.

POSITIONS ON THE FIELD

PUPIL: Now for some good advice for players on three separate areas of the field: forward, midfield, and defense. Try to remember this advice on the field, even though things may not always go as planned.

THE FORWARD POSITION

(Attacker and Striker)

In a game, there are usually two strikers who play up front in the team. Both will have a better opportunity to score goals than the rest of the team. Both strikers will need to combine with the midfield players who support them.

As a striker, you will often have your back to the opposition when you receive the ball. **Move away from your defender** and into a good position so that your teammates can play the ball **along the ground** to you. If you receive the ball in this manner and you are not sure what to do, **shield the ball, keep it at your feet,** but **look up;** only then can you decide your best option.

When you are going forward with the ball, try to keep the ball **close to your feet.** This will make the defender uncertain when to tackle. Keeping your **head up** will give you the confidence to vary your play and a quick burst of **speed** will put the defender behind you. Turn and move the ball into a space; this will give you more time to consider what to do next.

When you are going forward without a defender, this is a good time to use your speed. You could push the ball well forward, then run, but **steady yourself** as you approach the goalkeeper. Keep your **eye on the goal** then decide what to do: either shoot or go around him.

If you are close to, or in, the penalty area with the ball, try a shot. If you are in this same position without the ball, **move from space to space.** You must try to gain possession of the ball to stay in the game or score.

The best way for your team to go forward and still keep possession of the ball is by using **short, accurate passes.** Use one of your teammates to pass to, and then position yourself for the return ball.

If you are a striker, you will need to score goals with your head, so your **timing** and **forehead contact** are vital. You must also learn to defend, so close down the opposition, limit their space and chase.

When you do not have the ball, **do not run away** from your teammates. Do not expect them to pass a long ball to you over the defender's head unless, of course, you are certain of reaching it. Remember: a good defender will most likely win a 50-50 ball.

Scoring plenty of goals does not necessarily mean you are a brilliant player. If you are good at playing up front, move into midfield or even defense in order to gain more experience.

MIDFIELD

Usually, there are four players in midfield, but adult or more experienced teams often play with five. The midfield players will be in and around the center of the field, but they also cover the left and right side. During a game, these players will often support both the defense and attack. Other times they will be winning the ball in the midfield or masterminding forward play. Therefore, if you want to play midfield, you will have to be adaptable.

Most teams will have two types of midfield players: the ones who are clever on the ball and the ones who are stronger at tackling. A midfield player's first priority is to help the defense, especially in the first fifteen minutes of a game. This is the time to assess the opposition and make your presence felt in the game. Look to help your defenders, call to receive the ball, or get into a space.

If you are near to an opposing player who has the ball, move and limit his space. Hold your ground and, if he runs, go with him, force a mistake and chase. If you are a long way off from an opposing player who has the ball, pick up and mark another player. Always think defensively: you may need to chase him.

During a game, the ball will go back and forth many times, most likely in the air (especially in boys' games). Because of this, you must slow down—or even walk. Pace yourself for when you need to run. This will help you to calm down and allow you to see any mistakes. Remember: **slow your pace, this is not a race!**

If your team has possession of the ball, get into a space and then call. If you receive the ball, quickly control the ball, look up, then decide the best option to take. Remember that when you have the ball there is no need to beat your opposite players: moving quickly into a space and passing could prove to be the best option.

Do not attempt to beat an opponent in your own half of the field, or near the halfway line, unless you have clearly fouled your opponent. Always remember that possession of the ball is your top priority. Most youngsters play the ball up and down the field, but you must look to play the ball sideways. There will be players in space for this type of ball, so look for them.

Have you ever played in a game, five to a side? The field is a lot smaller and you need to be nimble. Well, be nimble when you are close to your opponents' penalty area. This will give you the time to hold the ball or make short passes, without any danger to your own team. Make this your practice area to gain in confidence on the ball.

If possible, play in all of the midfield positions, then try attack and defense.

DEFENSE

There are normally four defenders on a side, but some older or more experienced teams play with just three. The basic function of a defender is to stop the opposition reaching the goal and scoring; how they do this is another matter. Vision, speed, and timing all play an important role. Good defenders will also be skillful at passing the ball accurately, going forward, and supporting the attack. So, if you want to be a defender, don't think that you've just got to be a "stopper:" remember that you will need to defend when the opposition has the ball, so don't give the ball away!

There are usually two types of defender: the tall type and the fast type. If you have both of these assets, then defense may prove to be your specialty.

Although goalkeepers haven't previously been mentioned in this book, defenders must have a good understanding of them. You must know what they are doing, why they are doing it, and when they will do it. Keep an eye on a professional goalie and get to know how he plays.

As a general rule, intercepting the ball must be your first option. Whether the ball is in the air or on the ground, if you can get to it first, do so. Try to anticipate a pass or a move, and this will give you a good advantage over the opposition.

Push your team forward when they have possession of the ball, but make sure there is still cover at the back. Get a good idea of the ability of the opposition early in the game, especially the player whom you may need to defend against.

As a defender, you will often see the ball come toward you. This is an advantage, so make the most of it. Keep your eye on the ball and then decide your action. If you are going to mark a player, stay tightly with him, but do not tackle from behind. Be sure to keep your eye on the ball.

If an opposing player is coming toward you with the ball, move to one side and show him which way you want him to go. Always try to force him away from the goal, but stay on your feet and, if you tackle, make it a good one—firm and toward the ball. Always remember that any tackle must be sensible, and that you must make contact with the ball only—this way players will not get hurt and you will not be penalized.

If the ball comes to you in your own penalty area, just remember that, **if in doubt, put the ball out.** This type of play may not look very skillful, but may prove important. And, of course, be extra careful with your tackles in the penalty area.

Always look to support your team and call for the ball if

you are open. Always try to cover one of your players if he is going in for a tackle. Stay behind him so that, if he loses the ball, you are next in line to stop the opposition coming through.

As a defender, it is still important to show your talent on the ball. This position may, however, limit your time on the ball and cause you to rush your play on a number of occasions. You may not have the opportunity to experiment or go forward as much as you would like. As a young player, you need a great deal of ball possession in order to gain experience. Switch your position and play several games in midfield or attack throughout the season.

THE LAST WORD

PUPIL & TEACHER: As you will know by now, learning or teaching soccer skills is hard work. If you both keep at it, you should see that it is also very rewarding. Whether you reach the World Cup or the local park, if you are committed enough and if you try hard enough, your well-practiced soccer skills will allow you to shine above the rest.

INDEX